TREE OF LIGHT

A. N. Vogt

Gold Horizon Books

Copyright © 2024 by A. N. Vogt

Library of Congress Control Number: 2024902004

All rights reserved. This book or any portion thereof may not be reproduced or used in any manner whatsoever without the express written permission of the publisher except for the use of brief quotations in a book review.

Printed in the United States of America

First Printing, 2024

ISBN 979-8-9898137-0-4

Gold Horizon Books
Morgan Hill, CA 95037

CONTENTS

Prologue

Chapter 1: Link

Chapter 2: Edge of Consciousness

Chapter 3: Horizon of Time

Chapter 4: Elysian Fields

Chapter 5: Halls of Night

Chapter 6: Terminus

Chapter 7: Higher Light

Afterword

Dedication

At one spot the light grew solid as a brick wall, and like a piece of yellow Persian masonry, patterned in blue, daubed coarsely upon the sky the leaves of the chestnuts; at another, it cut them off from the sky towards which they stretched out their curling, golden fingers. Halfway up the trunk of a tree draped with wild vine, the light had grafted and brought to blossom, too dazzling to be clearly distinguished, an enormous posy, of red flowers apparently, perhaps of a new variety of carnation. The different parts of the Bois, so easily confounded in summer in the density and monotony of their universal green, were now clearly divided.

—Marcel Proust

Prologue

The invitation directs one, not to the academy, but to the fields within—where mental life flourishes. And walking along the garden paths, suddenly, within a pool's reflection, we notice the monastery before us: the place where we are taught that heart comes from heart.

And there is a sense that here we will be introduced to something rare, lying just beneath the earthen veil. To a theme, which is the spirit of philosophy, the tree of light.

Chapter 1

Link

✥

The truth is a description of existence. With its focus upon the world, the truth is in motion, is dynamic—shimmering. Like waves of light on waves of water; two travelers, shared events upon the stream of time. But when the truth is attuned to match the individual happenings of existence, it likens to the rain. And these drops which cover the Earth, being as numerous as they are, refract reality in so wide a spectrum, and in such unique ways, that one could mistake the waters of reality for having been formed in us, when it is rather we, who have been formed within them.

And perhaps one has already understood

through an inner voice of humility—a voice that though one may try to quell, nevertheless seems to remain, patiently waiting in the backroom of the mind, ever at the ready should we decide to enter her door and get to work upon a task that would confound even the most adept therapist. But as is the case on some days, when aligned with an unknown work pertinent to our development, humility rises from her seat and opens the door of consciousness to speak: "Truth could not have been designed singularly by us, for we are but one star in this universe ourselves."

And although it is a universe that in one's mind takes on a different form depending upon how it is perceived, the universe in its external and concrete reality possesses integrity—possesses an immunity to the imaginary worlds we create. It is not that reality is frail, it is that our perceptions are fickle, and the difference between these poles measures the distance the Homo sapien must traverse if it is to seat consciousness upon the throne of reality.

And that journey has already begun. The human species in its infancy makes connections with the world and grows up. Exploring the planet like a child crawling across their nursery, we advance outward. Gradually we come upon a different room, a special texture, a new kind of locomotion—and with each novelty visited, a parallel, internal vista is discovered.

The sensuous mind, attached to a foundation which is rotational, mobile, adaptable, is capable of projecting innumerable perceptions upon the deeper screen of thought—and we, whether unconsciously or consciously, perfectly or imperfectly: mirror nature. We "reflect" upon the objects accessible to us and represent them in our minds as a sort of reproductive process. It is a harmony that occurs, not simply by differing the note, but by changing the octave. Octaves apart, the melody of the universe has in accompaniment the instrument of consciousness, and it is through the gradual composition of a duet, that we, in what is perhaps closer, deeper than what objectivity could provide, form a bond with the universe.

But when the light of reality is caught by the instrument of consciousness, the ties that bind are revealed. Each drop of water experienced ties us to the experience of the whole. Within pure water, we experience all water—each of its instances within a single instance. Open your left hand and you will find a ticket granting access to a shortcut—the power to experience that same molecule whether it be contained within the rings of Saturn, or in the most remote regions of space billions of years ago.

But the drop cannot give one every *experience* of water. Water sipped in the summer of 1700, felt in the baths of Rome, or seen from another world. And so within your right hand you will find a key, which opens a single door, and only once. One's experience of the drop is singular, limited to the time and space in which that experience occurs. The ticket and the key—

these are what we should expect to find in a universe containing vast populations of poles, reverse charges, and opposites—we should expect to find that truth flows into and around these worlds, and knowledge, when reaching that celestial arena, attunes consciousness to not only itself, but to these greater scales of existence.

Chapter 2

Edge of Consciousness

❖

There is an inner light—which as it grows brighter, makes our vision all the clearer, and coming into view, is vision itself. An inward eye, an outer sight, the gaze turns in, turns out. A dual vision, and thought is the pendulum that swings between. Made to accompany life, the instruments of perception, however accessible, however swift their implementation may be—have been slowly built across time, successively.

Generation after generation, the successive work of family passes on to its descendants adaptations that render themselves in a unified form, a particular sculpture: a human being. Nature, the master sculptor, takes on its pupils, our father and mother, transmitting along two intertwined branches, stemming from the generational tree of which we are a part, a tree that is ultimately, one tree, a million pieces of "art", distilled down, and then flashing out—into a single, utterly unique living flower.

One of the great links between humanity and every other organism on the planet is this natural transmission of art. However, lineage is not guaranteed, and although the physical body will be reclaimed by nature, death is the crumbling of those structures which make "us" possible. Humility tells us that "a fallen leaf never turns green again" and again, "a fallen leaf never rejoins the tree from where it fell."

But perhaps it is possible to separate—to fall from life in the form of a seed. When an organism approaches, through this ever increasing gift of nature, this increasingly improved-upon art, a level of complexity which guides that life toward the unconscious perimeters within, up against the wall of unawareness, and finally beyond it—sensing the fact of existence, reaching the place where mind begins to study mind, and then begins to see beyond itself, to view life itself, and further still, comes to perceive the high stars of time and space—that organism is, in a very real sense, growing beyond itself, reaching out beyond itself.

Inner twilight fades before the dawn of existence, and exiting the dark world of unawareness, the roots of consciousness begin to weave into reality and provide the basis for a new life, where a fresh and flexible scaffold for becoming takes shape. It is through this extension of ourselves into the world, that the "spirit" of the sculpture, past the old bloodlines, may relay an intangible mark: the specific drive, personality, wisdom and passion of a being, onto those around us. And when this seed of mind falls upon the ground of another, when that spirit is accepted and adopted, given life within us, something that was the light of this individual—a lineage of light—is forged within us. Carried past death, their living light turns within us, the heart is changed, and a new person begins to form.

Like the tree which grows toward the sun, we may detect within us a greater star calling us to be transformed in the glow of another. Those who are on the road, who sense the wind of urgency, who reach for something higher, are awaiting this light—this transfer of life. And while this extension of life may bring with it even those qualities which are harmful, it is nonetheless through this wider conduit, where the rate of flow, and the content is set, not by family, but by mind, that the cure for what harms, might also be conveyed.

The sharing of life in all its fullness perpetuates it, expands it, sends life out not only horizontally across the Earth, but like all seeds of life which begin to grow—down, through time.

Chapter 3

Horizon of Time

✣

The lineage of light, flows through time and space, and as awareness combines with life, and this new way of being now just outside the original habitats of humankind is kindled on the slopes of reality, our activity in time begins to brighten in the night. Life moves with time, is of time, and beyond: to continue to exist, means a continued *freedom* to exist. We are free to exist, insofar as we *continue* to exist. The universe is free to exist! Each particle is free to exist. Time is ultimately one item, moving, opening, each event seamlessly arising from and transcending the former. The freedom to continue is not "contained" in time, rather this freedom is found in the very opening up of time itself. The freedom for all existence to continue is linked in to this continual, rising, expanding time. To be free to continue to exist, is to be unleashed, unchained from singular moments—it is a freedom that is ever moving, ever transcending, ever evading capture by time and space.

Existing is the voice of freedom. It is the evidence of freedom's existence. To experience existence is to experience freedom—it is an experience of "the opening", the unfolding, this singularly profound river of time.

To experience existence is to experience the fact of existence. But *freedom* could not be subjected to or pinned down by a fact, and the restrictions only amplify when we announce that we have understood this fact, that we have seized this fact. Could we really place "freedom" within the confines of a fact? How could we, lest what we hold immediately cease to be free. We can only speak of freedom as being continually uncapturable, a subtle acceptance that our terms simply fail in their attempts to enclose it. We must continue to adjust our language to freedom, and not attempt to rein freedom in or mold it to ourselves. Our language must match the ever-flow of it, and the openness of our own existence. Articulations and thoughts on freedom are not truly in alignment with what freedom is, unless they too are being unbound and set to match the free-flowing action of it. We cannot catch the ever-moving, but can opt to step into the stream. There is in a sense, a kind of letting go, and in the release it is as if *we* have been caught in the currents of the flow. Utilizing a rudimentary autonomy, we align ourselves with a freedom much more staggering than our own. It is a movement away from limiting thought, and into an open field, beyond a static "that is", and into the ever-moving river of being.

But are there not certain facts which are firmly fixed? They state precisely "that is" and simply do not alter. The combined length of two sides of an equilateral triangle *must* be longer than the remaining side. The circumference of a circle absolutely must be longer than its radius. How could facts of this nature be situated within the flowing waters of existence? Are not the mathematical requirements of the circumference and the radius a binding chain of some kind?

As time expands, what must be, continues to be. Even the chains are free to exist, through time. The factual universe compounds with the freedom of it—it is a continuum that has been, in all its combinational scope, unleashed. Even at the opposite edge of our perceptions: illusion, confusion, deception—these do not exist without being free to do so. Freedom moves behind and beneath, carrying them out into existence through time.

Can anything existing in time, truly be contained? Of history, we declare "it was", yet even this declaration—the moment it is made, it has gone. Despite the frozen past, the hand of the mind is moving—the hand that is trying to catch the river, happens to already be a part of it. Being's heritage, its history, is the hardened ice which remains behind when the sun of now surges across the sky of time, a hardened ground beyond which springs new water, and hardens as it springs, so that existence is always on the edge.

And moving upon the brink of time and proceeding into the future, is the heading set toward some end? Entropy begins to whisper of one possible fate for our universe: a seemingly inescapable, permanent diffusion of energy. Through the gradual distribution of heat, of molecular motion drawn slowly into disorder and finally down into an even calm, no longer could any work be extracted from the universe. No longer could there be any exchange of energy between a thermodynamic system and its surroundings. Although what remains continues to exist, matter would no longer be capable of performing any action pertinent to life. Will the seas of freedom fade beneath this entropic sun?

The freedom to exist matches the ever moving horizon of time. Thus even in entropy's final state, a vast horizon of existence lies ahead, its proportions matching the time which will continue to elapse. What might happen within a universe that continues to exist over an unfathomable amount of time? Outside the bounds of entropy, in the vast remainder of the universe, does not there still exist *possibility*? Freedom is keeping possibility alive, keeping alive hope.

But perhaps the eye of consciousness, as it follows the waves of time and light, can perceive a brighter hope. Entropy, the death of stars, or some other possible fate, spark the rising flame of awareness that all life in the universe—if nothing is changed, nothing is done—has a time limit. An awareness that something must be done, and perhaps not in the quiet acceptance of the monk, but with the faith of the outnumbered guard, having been trained by nature herself, not simply to survive, but to protect. The quest of consciousness, like time, at once opens upon—and toward the horizon.

Chapter 4

Elysian Fields

❖

Within the sanctum of the mind, nature fashions the guardian spirit, to move with time and freedom's flow, as if upon an ocean ship—that we might link our rising capacity to navigate, with the greater currents of existence.

And when we reach those shores of development suitable for cultivation, nature prepares the land, that flowers born of a lineage of light might be sown in different habitats of mind, within differing fields—so that life grows ever new. The mind bearing both the gardener and the garden within its contours of light, there lies within the potential for something almost Arcadian to take root in these fields, for life to spiral toward the upward roads and cosmic ends.

Field of Reason

The field of reason is that space where linguistic deliberation constructs and deducts congruent, logical, mathematical expressions of the experience of existence. An inner discourse which depicts the site of existence—it is a drawing made not merely to imitate, but allows the architect of experience to design something which can endure reality. A blueprint, which aligns us with those aspects of our world which can also be said to cohere, organize, and function geometrically.

Operating at breathtaking scales, within this

field reason is able to chart the history of galaxies, muse how they move through time and recede from one another, or map the intersection of physical events as invariable points within time and space. In physics, a human being mechanically aligns with nature—but it is at this rational turning point that we actually "square" thought with nature. It is the product of a genuine property of nature, and an organized representation of that property.

It is an alignment which multiplies thought, causes thought to surge within—and cascading down cliffs of mind the waters of reality begin to quench the questions and frame the answers, begin to synchronize conscious life, as if gradually bringing it into phase with the exterior world. While it is a terrain to which reason steadily orients our perceptions, to chart the land requires a second implement—the implement of choice.

Field of Will

We are drawn and propelled by the bow of reason to strike the target of our will—shot into the sky, to even land upon the moon. But however aerial its aims may be, the will finds its origins in the soil of an inner field. Beneath the terrain of instinct, our will lives under pressure, but growing in spite of this, ascends through the soil of suppression and breaks through the surface of our lives in response to a higher light. Despite the weight of earth pressing down, within the seed of will, within each one of us, lies an immense power—the power to act. To select from among the available possibilities, from among all those possibilities which lie before us, a route. To make a trail in one's life—to transform what is possible and make actual, by the hammer of will, a new creation. Each act carried out represents the actualization of that prior possibility, and brings into being a new configuration and sequence of events upon the expanding sea of time.

However limited the transaction, acts of will are an exchange upon the waters. Not simply of calm, for wind within the sails, but of captivity, for command. Directing not merely one's course, but who one is. Submit to will, character, and we begin to transition from character, to author. By strengthening and refining our technique, as nearly an act of premonition, we gradually come to anticipate our story. It is as if the will were so used to bringing into being the future, that it begins to predict the outcome.

As a species undergoes this metamorphosis from raw instinct to sunlit autonomy, becoming a people of will—action, creation and prediction, become increasingly stable, and dispositions begin to change, inclinations alter, and a new lens—a new dynamic of thought begins to form within.

Field of Imagination

The author, ready to act, ready to live, draws on their

imagination. That superterrestrial world, where the power of judgment has free-play with the objects of experience. Where continents of thought can be terraformed by the machinery of judgment—and every combination set within the manifold of experience is at its disposal. As both an engine of synthesis and an instrument of organization, the imagination can unite disparate concepts, or break the truth into shards of fiction.

But the machinery of imagination can also operate scientifically, mathematically, joining two truths together as if two atoms were just bonded into a molecule, or shift to unravel the unknown as a mystery is solved, and the shadowy figures of a crime are made visible.

When the engine of imagination is coupled to the wheel of will—when a creative force is applied to a mode of action, a storm of mind begins to gather. And when from the precipice the combination is unleashed, a new wind whirls across the Earth. But when it is combined with reason, the imagination becomes structured, almost contoured to the physical world of form, number, and pattern. Held in check by reason, and pushed forward by will, the tensions result in a kind of equilibrium, a balance of force perhaps required for the imagination to remain functional as an engine of modification within the physical world.

But the imagination is also a bridge spanning the gap between reasoning and acts of will, the creative power which determines how a rational thought may be carried into action, a catalyst, which does not obliterate the two in the making of one, but is a link uniting theory and practice. A door through which, hand in hand, reason and will step out into life.

The fields merge as one land—joined together within the kingdom of the mind, this tri-fold power re-orients, steadies, and grounds the composite human being—a human species, readying us for what lies ahead, waiting within the vast, unknown night. And while such power does not sum the human being, it measures the current of consciousness when arced toward those worlds positioned just beyond its reach. Toward the future world, where perhaps the fields within bloom so bright, their light breaks out across the surface, and recolors the landscape.

Chapter 5

Halls of Night

❖

Across the eras of development, the passes of life were seldom open—but humanity, still drawn up by the call of nature, traversed upon the mountainside. At each turn along the switchbacks of history, whole societies have fallen. Hope, diminished. But despite the unimaginable loss of life, our species has survived. And in pursuit of some unknown summit, a peak which remains shrouded from the light of conscious thought, we ascend, reaching milestones of development absolutely unfathomable in the past.

Cautiously, gently, but assuredly, Nature selects individuals to come upon the Earth. Composite beings, who ride upon the ridge of time, at the brink of the unfolding universe—and peering out across the horizon, begin to glimpse the sea of night. Ever on the edge, they continue to move through the universe as freed beings, rising from the darkness to freely act as participants of light—citizens of reality—and are linked together by a common bond: the fields of mind within.

And in the distance of time, when the fields flourish—at that point where satisfaction no longer is the goal, but the starting point, and when the focal point shifts from what is known, to what is unknown, the children of the Sun will leap into the darkness, and pursue what remains obscured within this unrealized world of night.

For here the pursuits of life are no longer

charged by instinct, but by a stable mind. And as the value of stability is realized, value itself, will gradually become the pursuit. Recognizing that there must be immense value lying beyond our isolated world, one senses the story is incomplete, and turns the page.

No longer *self*-oriented, the trajectory brings them into the titanic wake of the universe. Fortified by the past, they endure a thousand worlds, of mind and sky, and the kaleidoscopic input of experience, flowing in, charging within a vase of heart, finally forms a space and breaks forth across the horizons of mind. Fragmented, and rejoined, by the awesome endurance won in the past, they redraw the boundaries of thought as minds are remade again and again.

Cosmic adaptations that would have torn the

old humanity across its weakened seams now pull the threads tighter, strengthening the weave. Beyond mere survival, it is in this development of power that there will come a point when the energy of experience collides with the life behind it. The mind is like the sun. It is an engine which fuses together experience and character, thoughts and emotions, and results in the one acquiring something of the other, taking on a slightly different form, the auxiliary becoming further refined, or diminished. And when this fusion can be directed, like a sort of alchemy, will we not fashion something striking within us?

Continuing on into all those new horizons, after what seems like an unending journey upon some vessel into the night, we arrive at a completely unfamiliar station. A depot, where perhaps others have been before, and suddenly we understand that the train we are about to board, is to become the runaway train of our development. The route at once beyond and within, the sojourner is altered, and phased to match the course.

Chapter 6

Terminus

❖

When charting the development of a species and outlining those advances which have drastically altered its course, e.g. the development of tool building, writing, or technology, we discover that these adaptations are also augmentations to a broader, underlying mechanism: an apparatus of knowledge. A device which comes from Nature, and leads to Nature. Knowledge, at once a cumulative work of nature, and a distillation of that work—is fractaling within us; a shimmering crystal wherein thoughts look upon themselves—nature looks upon herself, in wonder.

And looking upon the crystal of knowledge, its contours set within, its scope, cosmic, it becomes apparent that this universe is bound to the physics by which it continues to exist, is relegated to spacetime ranges which are cast in an expanding "age" and "edge". However, it is precisely this limited, quantifiable cosmos, which can become known. As the apparatus of knowledge is advanced and as its content grows, it subtracts from the unknown universe. And were this process to continue for tens of thousands or millions of years beyond the conscious awakening of a species, where the acquisition of knowledge accelerates, not at a constant rate—rather, the further one travels, the faster they proceed—selecting those lessons which only decrease the need for more, so that in the workshop of the mind one skill acquired increases the range of another, eventually the limitations of the universe work in one's favor: for given the time, and the development, it is then but a matter of quantifying the quantifiable universe—of telling the true story behind the events which surround us.

It is through a complete knowledge of the cosmos, that all actions capable of being produced by it are revealed. To *know* that it can be done is to know that it *can* be done. Until an awareness, a knowledge of what is possible has been acquired, its realization remains beyond one's control. But from the moment one comes to know what is possible, it is as if the very seed of that possibility has just been sown within us. The power to work with all the available possibilities which lie before us, while striking, is not limitless. Amidst the many barriers, actualizations are limited to the total potential energy available within the universe. We have not come upon the shores of some infinite ocean; we have arrived at a well of power. While what can potentially be drawn up from nature is incredible, it will only ever match the quantitative reality within which we reside. And when those possibilities are channeled, directed toward life, their limitations carry over—the invincibility of life, blocked, by the total replicatory power available from which one might extend life. Utilizing the universe to sustain a species so that they might retain their identity over time, can never amount to immortal life—for the universe itself does not hold an endless repository of energy.

Mastery over life is not achieved through an an endless extension of it, but in perhaps acquiring the capacity to restore, to reforge life. It is an act of growth which does not merely extend, or accelerate the process, but initiates a transcendence of it—by selecting from a point of pure awareness exactly what, and who to become. It is a process taking place in rudimentary ways already, as perhaps a foreshadow, an allusion to our developmental potential. A kind of deliberate selection, that is not only adaptive, but progressive. The struggle to sow a field by hand, eased in time by equipment—by greater knowledge—mirrors the developmental process which will occur when tending to the fields of the mind.

And when the mind of an entire species has been recultivated—reengineered, fortified by knowledge—the option to act upon a new set of possibilities arises. Blooming from an aligned and enhanced mind, and imbued with a new imagination, the possibility of reorganizing the universe is suddenly revealed. The engineering power throttled only by what knowledge has shown to be impossible, the impossible, chiseled away by the hammer of reality.

It is through the quest of consciousness: a link to reality, a lineage of light, what time and mind reveal regarding the fate of life in our universe—and in what a universe of knowledge, ultimately bestows, that a profound alteration can now finally can be made.

Within the possible permutations to come, both the individual and the group may flow, each divining their own path, yet they will share in those elements, those arch-qualities, which have made the ascent possible. The inner stage upon which cosmic reengineering is made possible, is not wrought by the strength of the few—but marks the hour when the harmony of the species, a symphony of evolutionary archetypes, is configured into a musical key: unlocking at the summit of a new Olympus the golden gates, and the chimes are heard, as they step out onto the shimmering courtyard of the gods.

Chapter 7

Higher Light

❖

When like the trees, a species in all its diversity gradually grows together in harmony, life flourishes within the forest. The coalescence of the whole, and the individual, is one which cannot be replicated without understanding. We cannot grasp the whole without reference to its individual parts, nor can we understand the individual parts without reference to the whole. The one and the many united, the harmonic circle is the practical expression of peace. It is a circle, which inevitably forms enroute to that sacred mountain: the universe of knowledge. While the original code which directed our species was writ by the pen of survival, a work which perhaps pulls the species to fight even against some cosmic end, upon the harmonic heart there are now new symbols inscribed on its inner tapestry—a script of peace, etched in light—and a new score reads, "The narrative of life, anew."

And the sound of value, a spark of glory, an echo of character, resounds across the night as the curtains lift upon a new act, another story—the cosmos, reforged by light, sings out—and surely some being begins to hear the call as they examine the universe and witness its alterations. And perhaps something begins to stir within, moving them to act, to seek out that revolutionary light. Harmony, power, knowledge, expressed as the new dawn upon a grey horizon, the edge of the universe alit with the flame of an entire species, who break the fog not upon their accent, but from the summit of reality cast down through sky the unimaginable gift of life to those who still reside in the valleys.

And it was in the valleys as a young boy, that life seemed to me unmistakably valuable. Night after night, I would read each page on wildlife within those encyclopedias my parents would buy, studying every animal, every world, all the colors and details of their lives, until I felt I began to know these animals personally. On the next day, I would burst through the doors to the outside world, to run the trails and climb the trees. The forest alive in the morning and calm at night, the cycles a form of orientation to the natural environment.

But as the years went by and my interest in zoology began to fade behind the social scenery of those later years, it wasn't until while away at college when my mother called, that the death of my childhood cat suddenly washed over me with the waves of all those animals I had studied before, as if they had all been pronounced dead. What had once been my companion, a weaker being, died without the one it had comforted, and all those species which were confined to mere pages, then roused in me a commitment to life, a responsibility for life. And later whenever a plant would die, I would begin to feel, and even now, this immense sorrow because of the loss. Because the inner being senses that for these creatures a presence begins to fade, as time moves us further from their story. Time separates our stories—lives are cut.

But when a species is united in knowledge and power, would empathy not take hold? If even a book can spur a child and charge a single emotion to flower over the course of their life, would not these beings of light who behold in real-time the life of the universe, be moved to reach out their golden hand? Perhaps none have ever reached this point. Or perhaps some already have, and that which is set in motion is simply beyond our current grasp. And sometimes a change occurs gradually. Shifting the ancient energy which gave life to our universe beyond its predetermined course, from a destiny in darkness—through the life it has wrought, the mind it has taught, like winter before a new spring, to be transformed, in light. Whatever the means of metamorphosis may be, whenever the time of transformation in question, hope kindles, and faith stirs in the evening breeze—for those who would form a way beyond the final night. Who forge in time, a higher light.

Afterword

Time has opened the space required for life, and life has imprinted onto the fabric of reality art—designs born from the successive work of family, formed, from nature's dream. And melting down glaciers of unawareness into a sea of consciousness in the brightening sun of reality, life begins to reshape the world. And if somewhere there are beings nearing the forgeman's summit, or have long ago, the few who reach the pinnacle must be rare. For to reach that plane requires far more time, work, and chance to have elapsed than perhaps is common. Not every star has a planet, not every planet has life, not every ecosystem has sentience—and sentience is not guaranteed to achieve such extreme scientific mastery. If the developmental trajectory holds, yet the conclusion, unlikely, how *could* this come to pass? Is it a statistical necessity within grand chance, that of the multitudes, one species should rise so high? Or is it something more. Perhaps it is a question which cannot be fully addressed until much later in the story, for how could an explanation be given, when the context remains still so underdeveloped? We can only hope in the interim to receive a partial answer. Among the various powers, persons, and questions which frame our present lives—traced back through time and then drawn out again over the precipice of the future—which theme can draw us through the eye of the needle? The theme of light. Like the tree of life which links all species together within a common world, the world of reality is woven together in thought by an interconnected system of truth—far beyond text and lecture, past the political and scientific, turn toward the spirit of philosophy, the tree of light.

Dedication

Art can fashion a link between the hearts of sentient beings, and more than any one star, it is this constellation of life that depicts a narrative in time and space. In this spirit I dedicate my work, to those who differ in kind, but still seek some semblance of an answer when the links of light have caught on the edge of consciousness. When wading out into the unfolding tide of time, and the tempered mind is transfigured by that unknown night, its resolution…divine? To summon the diadem of thought and envision the crossing—'twas not formed by darkness, but out from it you've sprung into the golden dawn, and the higher light.

www.ingramcontent.com/pod-product-compliance
Lightning Source LLC
LaVergne TN
LVHW061530070526
838199LV00010B/443